Be the Magnet

YOFA® Essence Water Self Assessment Test

YOFA® Inner Alignment Methods
For Increasing Your Personal Magnetism
and Fulfilling Your Heart's Desires

By Rebbie Straubing, D.C.

YOFA®
New York

Disclaimer

This book has been written to provide information to help you live a joyful and satisfying life experience. The intent is to offer an uplifting approach to well-being. The purpose is to help you bring yourself into alignment with your inner truth, and to have you live a happier and more satisfying life experience. The products and processes described here are of a general nature and are meant to assist you in your quest for well-being. Rebbie is not a medical doctor or professional mental health counselor, and the methods offered here are not intended to be a substitute for advice from or treatment by a chiropractor, physician, therapist, or other health care professional. If you are in need of medical treatment or psychological counseling, you are encouraged to seek the services of a trained professional in those areas.

Every effort has been made to make this report as complete and accurate as possible. However, there may be mistakes in typography or content. Also, this report contains a simplified version of the YOFA® system of inner alignment and the associated products, services, and websites only up to the publishing date. Therefore, this report should be used as a guide – not as the ultimate source of YOFA® resources and information.

The intent of this book is to educate. The author and publisher do not warrant that the information contained in this report is fully complete and shall not be responsible for any errors or omissions. The author and publisher shall have neither liability nor responsibility to any person or entity with respect to any loss or damage caused or alleged to be caused directly or indirectly by this information.

If you do not wish to be bound by the above, please return this book for a full refund.

Material Connection Disclosure: You should assume that the author and publisher have an affiliate relationship and/or another material connection to the providers of goods and services mentioned in this guide and may be compensated when you purchase from a provider. You should always perform due diligence before buying goods or services from anyone via the Internet or offline.

Contents

Boost and Share Your Magnetism

▶ Send your friends a link to
www.BeTheMagnet.com so they can download
the ebook and get updates and extras.

▶ Download the ebook at
www.BeTheMagnet.com and print out as many
copies as you like.

▶ Buy more copies of the paperback book at
www.YOFA.net/magnet and give them away.

▶ Send your friends a link to
www.YOFA.net/magnet so they can buy the
book.

▶ Visit www.YOFA.net and get the free ecourse
"7 Secrets for Manifesting Your Heart's Desire."

How to Increase Your Magnetism With YOFA® Essence Waters

Y ou are a magnet. You are always attracting people, things, situations, and everything else you experience. In this small book, you will learn one method of increasing your magnetism so that you attract loving relationships, beautiful things, and situations that inspire your soul to sing. Of course, life always continues to offer its contrasting menu of experiences. But with this system, you attract more of what your heart desires. And when you do get lemons, you are more inclined to "make lemonade."

How It Works

Imagine two pieces of iron lying on a table, side by side. They look exactly the same. Same size. Same weight. Same color. You really cannot tell them apart. Except for one extraordinary property. One of these pieces of metal is a magnet. It has power. It can move things. It can draw things to itself. Its daily life contains a series of fulfilled desires as it draws to itself all that is resonant with its true nature.

Now imagine sitting on a bus full of people. They all look pretty much the same. Eyes, nose, mouth, limbs. Just ordinary people.

But now imagine that one of them (and I am talking about you) is a powerful magnet. One of them has the power to draw to himself or herself all that he or she wants.

In reality, all people are magnets, but most people do not know how to benefit from their magnetic nature. The difference between an ordinary magnet and a powerful magnet is simple. An ordinary magnet does not know it is a magnet and so it does not know that it is attracting what it is experiencing. It only attracts by unconscious habit, by default, and by the influence of mass consciousness.

A powerful magnet, on the other hand, recognizes and cultivates its own magnetism. It lives a degree of freedom that is unknown to the ordinary magnet. It lives the exhilaration of endlessly attracting the fulfillment of the desires of its heart.

A Revolution in Personal Magnetism

YOFA® Essence Waters represent a revolutionary breakthrough in the development of personal magnetism. Using these formulas on a regular basis can, little by little, completely change the trajectory of your life for the better.

The three primary YOFA® Essence Water formulas are based on the three axes of the physical universe (up/down, left/right, forward/backward). I explain the metaphysical counterparts of these axes in the book *Rooted in the Infinite*[1].

Which Formula is Right For You?

Most people will benefit from all three formulas. And these formulas can be used in a general manner without much attention to a specific intention.

---

1 You can look inside the book on Amazon at www.yofa.net/rootedintheinfinite

General Application

You can think of the general application of Essence Waters as giving your energy field a multivitamin. It helps across the board. This type of application of Essence Waters energizes your aura and fills in the gaps. It provides a general boost to your energetic field.

Specific Application

If you have ever had a natural health analysis, you know that a multivitamin is not always sufficient to make a correction. You may need to take certain specific nutrients, glandulars, herbs, or homeopathic remedies in order to bring your system into balance.

In addition to the general application of YOFA® Essence Waters, you can also use them in a much more intentional manner. At certain times, one particular formula may be especially therapeutic for you. To determine which formula and which level of YOFA jhe Sessions (more about *jhe* on page 34) would be best for you right now, consult the self-assessment test in the following section or ask your chiropractor to muscle test the remedies for you[2].

> ▶ Formula One aligns the Y-axis[3]
> ▶ Formula Two aligns the X-axis
> ▶ Formula Three aligns the Z-axis

Take the test on the next few pages and find out which formulas are best suited to you. On the recommendation pages you can see the best ways to use these formulas for the manifestation of your specific desires, goals, and intentions. Our understanding is constantly evolving so you can sign up for updates on new methods of application at www.BeTheMagnet.com.

2 Your chiropractor can contact me at rebbie@yofa.net to find out about ordering a test kit.
3 Each axis has a metaphysical counterpart in consciousness. The full explanation of the meaning of the axes can be found in the book *Rooted in the Infinite*. www.yofa.net/rootedintheinfinite

Inner Alignment and Personal Magnetism: Self-Assessment Test

Self-Assessment Part 1

Do you feel any of the following on a regular basis?
Check all that apply.

1. ☐ Low energy
2. ☐ Depression
3. ☐ Like you're on a treadmill
4. ☐ Difficulty sticking to a spiritual practice
   (meditation, prayer, etc.)
5. ☐ Desire greater spiritual awakening and awareness
6. ☐ Caught in a rut
7. ☐ Time is going too fast

Find the analysis of your answers to this question on the Formula One Recommendation Page.

Continue to Part 2 ⟶

Self-Assessment Part 2

Are you living with any of these conditions?
Check all that apply.

1. ☐ Physical illness (acute or chronic)
2. ☐ Physical injury (acute or chronic)
3. ☐ Symptoms of stress
4. ☐ Emotional overwhelm
5. ☐ Hypersensitivity

Find the analysis of your answers to this question on the Formula Two Recommendation Page and use the Meric chart[4] to help you understand where to apply the remedy.

Continue to Part 3 ➞

---

4 You can access the Meric chart at www.BeTheMagnet.com/charts.

Self-Assessment Part 3

Do you experience any of the following obstacles?
Check all that apply.

1. ☐ Procrastination, clutter, blockage, frustration.
2. ☐ Difficulty finding your soul mate.
3. ☐ Conflict in your primary relationship.
4. ☐ Conflicts with family, friends, co-workers, etc.
5. ☐ Financial stress, lack, worry.
6. ☐ Difficulty acquiring desired possessions.
7. ☐ Blocked artisitc expression.

Find the analysis of your answers to this question on the Formula Three Recommendation Page.

Self-Assessment Analysis: YOFA® Formula One Recommendations

The following uses for YOFA® Formula One Essence Water correspond to the numbers of the answers you checked on Part 1 of the Self-Assessment. For example, if you checked answer #7, "Time is going too fast," you would read #7 below, "Slow Down Time."

1. **Energy** - To replace fatigue with energy and vitality.

   ▶ Recommendations: Apply to top of head, root (through clothing) soles of feet, sternum, above belly button, pubic bone, back of wrists, front of ankles. Wear pendant. Jhe Sessions: active, inner circle, or Y axis.

2. **Lift Spirits** - To replace depression with eagerness and happiness.

   ▶ Recommendations: Apply to top of head, root (through clothing) soles of feet, sternum, above belly button, pubic bone, back of wrists, front of ankles. Wear pendant. Jhe Sessions: active, inner circle, or Y axis.

3. **Present Time Awareness** - To be in the now and appreciate every moment.

   ▶ Recommendations: Apply to top of head, soles of feet, above belly button, pubic bone, root (through clothing) back of wrists. Wear pendant. Jhe Sessions: active, inner circle, or Y axis.

4. **Spiritual Practice** – This formula helps you along in your spiritual practice. Meditation, prayer, etc. Lessens resistance, helps you remember, and makes it more appealing to go within.

> ▶ Recommendations: Apply to top of head, soles of feet, root (through clothing), third eye, throat (externally at front of neck), sternum, above belly button, pubic bone. Wear pendant. Jhe Sessions: active, inner circle, or Y axis.

5. **Spiritual Qualities** – Awaken, deepen, and gain greater access to Divine Love, transcendent wisdom, bliss, and direct mystical perceptions of reality.

> ▶ Recommendations: Apply to top of head, soles of feet, third eye, and throat (externally at front of neck). Wear Pendant. Jhe Sessions: active, inner circle, or Y axis.

6. **Clean Slate** – When you feel caught in a rut, doing the same old things and getting the same old results over and over, this formula helps you reawaken to every moment as a clean slate.

> ▶ Recommendations: Apply to top of head, soles of feet and root (through clothing). Wear Pendant. Jhe Sessions: active, inner circle, or Y axis. Also see Formula Three item #1 "Breakthrough."

7. **Slow Down Time** – When time seems to be racing by, this formula helps you fit more into your day and fill each moment more fully with life.

▶ Recommendations: Apply to top of head and root. Wear Pendant. Jhe Sessions: active, inner circle, or Y axis.

Formula One is a Y-Axis remedy currently available in the following forms:

___ Spray   ___ Drops   ___ Pendant

Formula One works synergistically with the YOFA jhe Sessions (You can find out more about the remote inner alignment sessions called "YOFA jhe Sessions" on page 34.)

Self-Assessment Analysis: YOFA® Formula Two Recommendations

The following uses for YOFA® Formula Two correspond to the numbers of the answers you checked on Question 2 of the Self-Assessment. For example, if you checked answer #1, "Physical illness (acute or chronic)," you would read #1 below. Also, check the Meric chart for additional areas of application.

1. **Energy of Physical Healing*** – This formula promotes energy flow and fluid communication throughout the body. It assists your innate intelligence in expressing as optimal physical functioning and brings a feeling of vitality.

   ▶ Recommendations: For general well being, apply above belly button, at throat (externally at front of neck), and pubic bone. Wear pendant. Jhe Sessions: active, inner circle, or X axis.

   ▶ Bring Light to Illness – In case of illness, also apply to related spinal segment (see Meric chart at www.BeTheMagnet.com/charts). If you cannot reach the back, apply to the corresponding area on front of body. You can also apply directly to the area that needs help. Wear pendant. Jhe Sessions: active, inner circle, or X axis.

2. **Rapid Healing of Injury*** – This formula promotes the flow of healing energy and intelligence to the injured part for more rapid, full, and proper healing.

▶ Bring Light to Injury - In case of injury, apply above belly button, at throat (externally at front of neck), and pubic bone, on top of head, and to the area of spine that connects to the injured part. Also, apply directly to the injured part.

3. **Stress*** – Whether work related, money related, or any other type of stress, this formula acts like a resting place. It promotes relief from tension and opens a space for the feeling that all is well.

▶ Recommendations: Apply to the top of shoulders, third eye, above belly button, and back of knees. Wear pendant. Jhe Sessions: active, inner circle, or X axis.

4. **Emotional Stability*** – Where emotions are out of balance, this formula promotes energy balance and a feeling of ease.

▶ Recommendations: Apply to third eye and above belly button. Wear pendant. Jhe Sessions: active, inner circle, or X axis.

5. **Personal Empowerment*** – Where hypersensitivity is producing feelings of vulnerability and sensory overwhelm, this formula has a soothing effect. It strengthens the template of stability and increases the energy capacity of your system. The result is a feeling of personal empowerment and groundedness.

▶ Recommendations: Apply above the belly button, at throat (externally at front of neck), and back of knees. Wear pendant. Jhe Sessions: active, inner circle, or X axis.

Use the nerve supply chart at www.BeTheMagnet.com/charts for the levels to spray Formula Two to enhance the energy body's natural ability to support healing.

Formula Two is an X-Axis remedy currently available in the following forms:

____ Spray   ____ Drops   ____ Pendant

Formula Two works synergistically with the YOFA jhe Sessions. (You can find out more about the remote inner alignment sessions called "YOFA jhe Sessions" on page 34.)

*Disclaimer: This is offered for general well being and does not diagnose or treat medical or psychological conditions.

Self-Assessment Analysis: YOFA® Formula Three Recommendations

The following uses for YOFA® Formula Three correspond to the numbers of the answers you checked on Question 3 of the Self-Assessment. For example, if you checked answer #2, "Difficulty finding your soul mate," you would read #2 below, "Attract Soul Mate."

1. **Breakthrough** - To move past obstacles and get things done. For success. To organize and get rid of clutter. To move past procrastination.

   ▶ Recommendations: Apply to back of wrists, front of ankles, and third eye. Wear pendant. Jhe Sessions: active, inner circle, or Z-axis.

2. **Attract Soul Mate** - The Universe is already bringing you together. This formula helps you rendezvous, recognize each other, and bring the relationship into manifestation.

   ▶ Recommendations: Apply above belly button, at center of sternum, at third eye, at pubic bone. Wear pendant. Jhe Sessions: active, inner circle, or Z-axis.

3. **Harmonize Romantic Relationship** - In marriage and romantic partnerships, conflicts and irritations may arise over time. This formula re-tunes you to the love and harmony of the first "falling in love" feelings.

► Recommendations: Apply to center of sternum. Wear pendant and/or place pendant on night stand. Jhe Sessions: active, inner circle, or Z-axis.

4. **Harmonize All Relationships** – From family relationships, to co-workers, to friends, or even to humanity in general, this remedy helps bring you into alignment with others in a way that promotes respect, kindness, and authentic compassion and connection. With friends it can produce laughter and fun. With co-workers it can augment respect and cooperation.

► Recommendations: Apply to third eye, sternum, root (through clothing). Wear pendant. Jhe Sessions: active, inner circle, or Z-axis.

5. **Attract Money** – You have already put out the call vibrationally for more money. And the Universe is eager to provide it to you. You may have inner conflicts about your worthiness or about whether or not it is right for you to even ask for more money. These conflicts block the manifestation even though the Universe is abundant and does not need to take away from anyone else in order to deliver to you. This formula helps bring you into alignment with your desire for joyful abundance and manifestation.

► Recommendations: Apply to third eye, above belly button, at pubic bone, at root (through clothing) on back of wrists and on front of ankles. Wear pendant and/or place in wallet or purse. Jhe Sessions: active, inner circle, or Z-axis.

6. **Attract Material Things** – When you are looking to attract/manifest something specific, this formula helps you rendezvous

with the things you seek. It can be as major an acquisition as a house or car. It can be as simple as the right hair product or comfortable shoes.

> ▶ Recommendations: Apply to third eye, throat (externally at front of neck), center of sternum, root (through clothing), and front of ankles. Wear pendant. Jhe Sessions: active, inner circle, or Z-axis.

7. **Expression of Talents** – Painters, sculptors, singers, musicians, dancers, actors, writers, and artists of all kinds (professionals and amateurs) rely on direct access to inspiration and a clear channel for its expression. The living of life itself can be your art. This formula helps bring you into alignment with the flow of inspiration that expresses as spectacular originality and skillful creation.

> ▶ Recommendations: Apply to third eye, sternum, above belly button, pubic bone, front of ankles. Wear pendant and/or place it in studio area. Jhe Sessions: active, inner circle, or Z-axis.

Formula Three is a Z-axis remedy currently available in the following forms:

___ Spray   ___ Drops   ___ Pendant

Formula Three works synergistically with the YOFA jhe Sessions. (You can find out more about the remote inner alignment sessions called "YOFA jhe Sessions" on page 34.)

Pendant Combinations and Placements for Maximum Effectiveness

1. Mutual Attraction

Whether you want to attract your soul mate or you want to bring more love and passion into your existing relationship, Formula Three is the vial to wear around your neck, carry in your pocket, or keep in your purse. You can also keep one of these on your night table. To add a "backbone" to your relationship quest so that you always maintain your relationship with your inner guidance as primary, add Formula One. This is especially valuable if you tend to lose yourself in relationships. To increase your vitality and physical attractiveness, add Formula Two to the mix. With all three vials charged with your heart's desire, you are a true love magnet. The Mutual Attraction Bundle includes one Formula One pendant, One Formula Two pendant and one Formula Three pendant.

2. Balancing Act

When Life is overwhelming and you feel you are losing your balance, keep Formula Two nearby. If it is work that has you stressed, place a Formula Two vial on your desk. If the stress has reached a point of causing physical symptoms, wear the Formula Two pendant around your neck or carry it in your pocket or purse. To add a dimension of clearing the path before you, smoothing out your relationships with others, and generally reducing the stress reaction to the bumps in the road, add a Formula Three vial to your day. The Balancing Act Bundle includes one Formula Two pendant and one Formula Three pendant.

3. Pennies From Heaven

"Every time it rains it rains pennies from heaven...You'll find your fortune falling all over town."[1] You can use the combination of Formula One and Formula Three to find your fortune everywhere you look. Increase your natural prosperity. Tap into universal abundance. Carry these two vials in your wallet to energetically attract money. Keep them where you pay your bills. Keep a formula Three vial near your checkbook. If you are in business, keep one near your appointment book or cash register. Adding the Formula One vial supports your awareness of Infinite Abundance. The Pennies From Heaven Bundle includes one Formula One pendant and one Formula Three pendant.

---

1 From the lyrics to *Pennies From Heaven* by Johnny Burke

There are Only 3 Kinds of Desires

You may think you have way more than three different kinds of desires. And of course you would be right. You may want a new car or a new house. You may want to find the love of your life or to rekindle the love in your marriage. You may be seeking physical healing and that alone contains so many different types of desires.

There are desires for harmonious family relationships, attractive physical appearance, strength and vitality, clothing, jewelry, and almost all the things you find down the aisles of your favorite stores. The list goes on and on.

So, yes, we could make lists of categories of your multitude of desires, but we won't. You will find that all your desires fit perfectly into this naturally occurring, simple system of three categories.

The "Aha!" that occurs when you see the elegance of this natural system of three categories becomes the first giant step toward the fulfillment of all your desires.

The First Step Toward Fulfillment: Joyful Journey

Before you can have a fulfilled desire you must have a joyful journey. (Please read that sentence at least 3 times before proceeding.)

Defining Terms

By a "fulfilled desire" I mean that you are joyful in the receiving of what you have asked for. That means that you not only got the house, but you are still loving the house as you live in it. It means that you not only found your soul mate but that you are joyful each time your eyes meet.

So you can see that a fulfilled desire is a two-part thing. It is not just a manifestation. It is a joyful manifestation. To be clear, if you get the house and it only brings you more problems, we will not be calling that a fulfilled desire.

The Role of the Joyful Journey

In order to arrive at a fulfilled desire, it helps to take the path of the joyful journey. Here are a few reasons why:

1. By practicing joy on your journey, you have the skill of joy when you arrive at your fulfillment. By practicing joy as you search for your house or your soul mate or your strong body, you will more naturally find joy in those fulfillments. Conversely, by practicing discontent and dissatisfaction on your path to your desire, you will more naturally find discontent and things to complain about in your new fulfillment.

2. By practicing joy on your journey, the journey itself becomes the fulfillment since the reason you want the fulfillment is for the joy.

3. By practicing joy on your journey, your release resistance to the lack and you become a vibrational match to your desire and attract it more quickly, more purely, and it arrives in a more satisfying form.

Why Only 3 Kinds of Desires?

By understanding all your desires as one of, or a combination of, these 3 types of desires, you increase your access to the joyful journey.

This system makes all your desires mutually beneficial. That means that as you start attracting the fulfillment of one desire, you automatically draw to you the fulfillment of the others, too.

The way most people engage with their desires holds those desires as individual conflicting forces. This has a de-magnetizing effect. The desires cancel each other out. For example, if you want more money, you must work more and spend less time with your family. If you spend more time with your family you must work less and make less money. If these statements of competition between desires seem accurate to you, you are keeping your desires in conflict.

This typical, default way of holding your desires can leave you scrambling around, reaching for this and reaching for that, spreading yourself thin, getting this but losing that in the process. When you focus your attention on one desire you seem to lose hold of the others. This can quickly turn into bitterness and resentment. Quite the opposite of the joyful journey!

Simplicity to the Rescue

Fortunately, there are 3 kinds of desires in this world we live in. They are built into our three dimensional world and they are programmed into our bodies. They occur in nature and they form the structure of our consciousness. Once you come into awareness of these three kinds of desires and you cultivate your alignment with them, each desire strengthens the others.

That means that as you focus on your relationships, you are also attracting material abundance. As you focus on spiritual awareness and inner peace, you are also attracting your soul mate or attracting customers to your business, or harmony in your family.

Instead of your desires canceling each other out and competing for your time and attention, we find the opposite here. Your desires work in harmony with each other and every effort you make toward one desire supports the fulfillment of all the others.

What Are the 3 Kinds of Desires?

The three kinds of desires can be thought of as movements of energy. Desires move in certain directions. Some desires have an energy that moves in the up/down axis. Some desires move side to side, and others move forward/backward.

Those are the three basic categories of desires and you will find that all your desires fit into this simple picture. These three directions form the basis of our physical universe. They reflect the three dimensions of our world.

Since these three dimensions exist in nature, and since we participate in nature in every aspect of our lives, we can make our journey much more joyful and harmonious by tuning to this simple reality.

Spiritual Desires

Spiritual desires run in the up/down axis. These are desires for connection to God, spiritual awareness, inner peace, unconditional love, transcendent wisdom, and other manifestations of connection to Divinity.

Since these desires run in the up/down axis, let's refer to these as Y-axis desires. You can increase your Y-axis alignment with Formula One Essence Water.

Personal Balance and Well-Being Desires

The second category of desire is for your personal well-being. You may think of this as the category of healing. These are desires for physical vitality, strength, and perfect body functioning. This is also where we find the desire for balanced and stable emotions. These are the natural desires that arise within you for the well-being of your personal system of life, body, mind, and emotions.

Since these desires run in the side to side axis, let's refer to these as X-axis desires. You can increase your X-axis alignment with Formula Two Essence Water.

Joyful Manifestation Desires

The third category of desire includes all your relationships, your finances, your material possessions, and your expression into the world. This includes your art, your work, and all the activities that make up your unique journey. Money, family, friends, romance, school, work, play, houses, cars, boats, jewelry, clothing, you find all this in the third category of desire.

Since these desires run in the forward/backward axis, let's refer to these as Z-axis desires. You can increase your Z-axis alignment with Formula Three Essence Water.

3 Kinds of Fulfillment That Bring Joy

Now that you understand all your desires as fitting into one of the three categories, you can see that there are basically three types of fulfillment in life.

In addition to living in a three dimensional world of nature, we also find metaphysical counterparts for these three dimensions in consciousness. (There are more dimensions in consciousness which we can access once we align these three.)

When any one of these three axes comes into alignment it opens the flood gates for the fulfillment of the desires that live on that axis.

Aliveness, Awareness, Awe-Filled Ecstasy

The first category of fulfillment (Y-axis) re-awakens your love of life. It is here that we find the ecstatic mystical experiences and all the other forms of joy that ring that same tone.

This awe-filled ecstasy is the joy that comes from direct access to Infinite Consciousness.

Your upright spine is the home of your Y-axis, or spiritual, desires. It is also the gateway for the other two categories of desire. This axis must be in alignment for all three categories of fulfillment.

When the vertical energy flow is clear and moving smoothly, you gain access to the fulfillment of your spiritual desires.

For example:

1. Meditation and prayer, or whatever your spiritual practice may be, become more pure and offer greater connection to God and spiritual awareness.

2. Deeper levels of inner peace come into your reach.

3. You gain access to the blessing of unconditional love.

4. You can meet the challenges and joys of your life with the equanimity of transcendent wisdom.

5. There are more manifestations of connection to Divinity than I can mention here, and you will sense their sacredness as they unfold.

In addition to the overtly spiritual desires that can be fulfilled through this alignment, there are other benefits to the Y-axis energy movement:

1. Spiritual upliftment is a dominant characteristic of this axis. If you feel heavy, tired, depressed, or in any way dragged down by life, the Y-axis alignment promises the solution to your problems. It puts pep in your step and lifts your spirits.

2. The Y-axis also provides the pathway for the energy to flow into the other two axes. If you seek healing or joyful manifestation, the first place to start is with the vertical fulfillment. Attempting healing or manifestation without tending to the Y-axis first is like installing a beautiful new Jacuzzi in a house with no plumbing. If there is no water running into it, it is

basically useless. The Y-axis alignment flows energy to the other two axes.

The fulfillment that comes via the vertical is uplifting and globally beneficial for your whole system. It brings the joy that is of the quality of ecstasy. Formula One promotes this fulfillment.

Wholeness, Wellness, Happiness

The second category of fulfillment (X-axis) brings your entire system into balance and wholeness. It is here that we find profound, and at times instant, healing of physical and emotional dis-ease. The remembering of the whole is an extraordinary experience that cannot be conveyed in words. It can leave a trail of seeming miracles as ailing body parts can come back to proper functioning and painful emotional patterns can dissolve into complete nothingness[1].

While this alignment can at times provide instantaneous healing, more often it is a process of "peeling the onion." Each phase of the fulfillment brings new balance, new insights, new relief, and a new platform for the next fulfillment.

The fulfillment that comes via the X-axis is soothing, offers relief of physical and emotional pain, and offers rest for the weary traveler who needs time to recover from life's harsh storms. It brings the relaxed joy that is of the quality of contentment. It has the feeling of "My cup runneth over." Formula Two promotes this fulfillment.

---

1 While miracles can and do happen as a result of YOFA® Inner Alignment methods, these are not guaranteed nor are they typical. This is not meant to diagnose nor treat medical or psychological conditions Please consult your health care professional. YOFA® methods work on a vibrational level and allow your own natural healing forces to flow where they might have been blocked. All healing that occurs in this system is due to the body's and mind's natural ability to heal itself.

Joyful Journey, Fulfilling Manifestation, Loving Relationships

The third category of fulfillment (Z-axis) forms the joyful journey. It is here that we find the relationships that give life meaning, the forms of expression that keep life force flowing, and the material means to live a life of beauty, grace, and generosity.

There are so many potential manifestations in this broad category that it can be very helpful to realize that they all distill down to the journey of your unique life. In this phase, while you are acquainting yourself with the three categories of fulfillment, you can release your tight focus on specific desires and get a sense of the forward movement of your "chariot." Feel the rhythm of the steps that move you forward. Feel the exhilaration of the breeze on your face as it lets you know you are on a great and unique adventure.

The manifestations that come via the Z-axis, such as money, romance, material wealth, and so on, are often sought after from an angle that can produce suffering. That is why so many spiritual paths recommend releasing this type of desire all together. These paths more often recommend vows of poverty and chastity rather than methods for attracting wealth and relationships. But since this Z-axis dimension is built into you as a reflection of nature, giving up these desires can be very difficult to do.

That is why, in this system, rather than trying to let go of these Z-axis desires, you are harmonizing them so that they become an integral part of the ever-evolving joy of your life. Joy is the true nature of these desires. And through your inner alignment, their joy expresses in the fulfillment of your journey.

The fulfillment that comes via the Z-axis brings the joy that is of the quality of a thrilling passion for life. Formula Three promotes this fulfillment.

3 Magnetizing Methods That Bring Joy & Fulfillment

Now you see that you have three categories of desires that run along three axes:

- ▶ Spiritual (up/down: Y-axis)
- ▶ Healing (side to side: X-axis)
- ▶ Joyful Journey (forward/backward: Z-axis)

You also see that each axis brings its own type of fulfillment and each fulfillment brings its own type of joy.

Since each one of these axes can allow energy to flow or can block the flow of energy, we can get a big, confusing mix of manifestations. We sit there scratching our heads because we thought we knew how to do this manifestation thing but it didn't work.

Y-Axis Flow

When your energy flows well in the Y-axis, you become a powerful magnet for spiritual awakening. This can mean that you are attracting the thought forms or energetic alignments that promote spiritual awareness. In addition to opening you to direct mystical experience, this alignment can attract the teachers, books, centers, and other events on your journey that nourish your spiritual awakening.

X-Axis Flow

When your energy flows well in the X-axis, you become a magnet for optimal personal functioning of body, mind, and emotions. Again, this refers both to the direct balancing and functioning of your system as well as to attracting people, methods, information, and products that can help you.

Z-Axis Flow

When your energy flows well in the Z-axis, you become a magnet for all the people, things, money, and experiences that your heart desires. You become aligned for a joyful journey and you attract all the specifics that thrill you personally.

Let's look at three ways of increasing your alignment and your magnetism. These will work for any and all of the three axes. These methods work individually and in any combination. Each method strengthens the others.

Magnetizing Method #1:
Inner Alignment Meditation

When you sit down to meditate, you come into direct relationship with your vibration.

There are many different forms of introspection that are all called meditation. For the purpose of coming into alignment with your essence, purifying your vibration, increasing your magnetism, and living a fulfilling life journey, I will be referring to the YOFA® system of inner alignment when I speak of meditation in this book.

The exercises in the book *Rooted in the Infinite* form the basis of the meditation practice to increase your magnetism. As you work with the book you gain greater insight into the nature of the three axes. You also learn how to increase your magnetism by aligning each axis with precision.

The YOFA® system of inner alignment can be learned by anyone and can be done by anyone. Since I teach the system in the book *Rooted in the Infinite*, you have access to the conceptual framework as well as the actual meditation training from the comfort of your own home. You do not need to go anywhere to study this. You can greatly increase your magnetism by simply following the instructions in the book.

To help you move quickly and deeply into the meditation process, you can use the meditation recordings available at www.RootedintheInfinite.com/the-meditation-recordings so that you don't have to read while you engage in the exercises.

Using meditation as a magnetizing method breaks old patterns of self sabotage and replaces them with powerful, beneficial attractive forces.

This method can even reach into ancestral energetic misalignments that have been passed to you and may be blocking your magnetism in ways that you are not aware of. The wonderful thing is that as you untangle these patterns through your meditation, you bring ease and healing to your ancestral line and soothe those who came before you while empowering those who will come after you.

This meditation practice offers a life long journey of inner exploration. It can also be used as preparation for any other type of meditation because it acts as a connector between your active day-to-day mind and your more quiet meditative awareness.

If you do any other type of sitting or movement meditation, or if you plan on beginning some type of meditation, use the YOFA® inner alignment exercises to amplify the benefits you receive from your other forms of practice.

The magnetism that you cultivate with YOFA® meditation grows and matures with time. You are cultivating your own energy field and your harvest reflects the purity of your efforts. The joy and fulfillment from this magnetizing method can be directed toward different axes. For example, if you seek healing, you can focus your meditation on the X-axis and find relief, wholeness, healing, and contentment regardless of conditions.

Magnetizing Method #2:
Remote Inner Alignment Sessions

Whether you choose to do the inner alignment meditation exercises or not, you can increase your magnetism with the YOFA® inner alignment sessions (YOFA jhe Sessions).

While the meditation practice requires effort, the remote sessions require no effort at all. You do absolutely nothing. (I do all the work.)

Here is how it works.

Since we are all connected, we have the ability to promote healing and balance in each other. And since we are energy beings, we can receive a beneficial influence without physical contact.

You can think of your membership in the YOFA® remote inner alignment sessions as a "wireless" connection that increases your magnetism. This is one way to cultivate your inner alignment and increase your magnetism that does not require your conscious effort. This is beneficial because, since it is not employing your conscious mind, it bypasses your typical blocks and patterns of self sabotage, should you have any. It is also perfect for those who are too busy or who, for any other reason, prefer not to meditate. Of course, the best arrangement is to do both.

I call these sessions the YOFA jhe Sessions. By now you probably know that "jhe" is pronounced "jee" (rhymes with "key") and it stands for joyful harmonious expressiveness. There are different levels of participation. You can find the one that works best for you.

Once your name is on the jhe list, I begin doing sessions for you. Some people feel the sessions quite distinctly. Others feel nothing at all. Either way is fine. When you get the email update from the session, simply contemplate its meaning for you and then go about your business. That is all there is to it.

Little by little you will feel, see, and notice signs of your increased magnetism. The membership is ongoing because, just like meditating, this process of inner alignment gets more profound the longer you do it. And just like brushing your teeth, or bathing, this process cleans and clears the energetic debris that accumulates from daily life.

The jhe sessions have helped people with a broad range of physical, emotional, financial, spiritual, and relationship problems. The most common, and usually instant, benefit that most people feel is an experience of lightness.

If you are serious about increasing your magnetism, the YOFA jhe Sessions are for you. They get deep into places that can be difficult to access through other methods. These sessions are even helping kids on the autism spectrum[1] to hug their parents more, speak more words and with more clarity, and feel happier. Imagine what they can do for you.

---

1 Download the YOFA Unconditional Love Project research report *Words & Hugs* at www. UnconditionalLove.info/research

Magnetizing Method #3:
YOFA® Essence Waters

The third magnetizing method is something you can wear, carry with you, place in strategic locations, and apply to your body and energy field.

These essence waters are homeopathically potentized to hold the vibration of the axis alignments.

By spraying and/or wearing Y-axis water (Formula One), you are effortlessly tuning yourself to spiritual awareness all day long.

Spray and/or wear X-axis water (Formula Two) for healing.

Spray and/or wear Z-axis water (Formula Three) for joyful manifestation of successful action, loving relationships, money, etc.

All three formulas promote a happy feeling and both the X and Z waters contain a Y-axis component so that they can work fully on their own. Use the self-assessment test that begins on page 8 to find out the best ways to use the Essence Water Sprays in your daily life.

To augment the power of these formulas, set an intention, speak or write an affirmation or prayer, and/or see your desired outcome in your imagination as you spray, wear, or place your remedies.

Summary

▶ There are three dimensions in our physical world.

▶ There are three corresponding dimensions in consciousness.

▶ There are three kinds of desires, one for each of the three dimensions.

▶ There are three kinds of fulfillment. One for each kind of desire.

▶ There are three main YOFA® Essence Water Formulas. One for the fulfillment of each kind of desire.

▶ There are three main YOFA® methods for bringing yourself into alignment with your essence to increase your magnetism.

▶ The three main YOFA® methods are:

>   ▶ YOFA® Inner Alignment Meditation
>   ▶ YOFA jhe Sessions
>   ▶ YOFA® Essence Waters

▶ By increasing your magnetism, you cultivate the joyful journey to, and the fulfillment of, all three categories of desire.

▶ You can learn the YOFA® Inner Alignment meditation method from the book *Rooted in the Infinite*.

▶ You can sign up to receive YOFA jhe Sessions and order YOFA® Essence Waters at www.BeTheMagnet.com/manifest

Where to Spray

The Self-Assessment test recommendations on pages 11-19 tell you where to spray each formula for your desired results. Here are more detailed descriptions of the spray locations.

Note: You can always spray through clothing. It is best to spray while standing or sitting upright. Formula Two can be applied while lying down.

1. Top of head - Spray down onto top of head.
2. Third eye - Spray the point between and above the eyebrows. (Close eyes so spray goes only on skin.)
3. Throat - Spray externally on front of neck.
4. Top of shoulders - Spray downward on the "shelf" of both shoulders.
5. Center of sternum - The sternum is the "breast bone" or the bone at the center of your chest. Spray right on the center of this area.
6. Back of wrists - Spray on both wrists on the same side of hand as fingernails.
7. Above belly button - You also have the option to spray right at the level of the belly button (through clothes).
8. Pubic bone - This is the bone several inches directly below the belly button.
9. Root (through clothes) - Hold the spray bottle between the knees and then move about halfway up the thighs. With the spray bottle between the legs spray directly upward.
10. Back of knees - Spray directly onto the back of both knees.
11. Front of ankles - Spray the point where the foot meets the front of the leg. Do this for both ankles.
12. Soles of feet - Spray on soles of both feet. You can also spray the soles of your shoes or spray into your shoes.

Spray Locations

1. Top of head
2. Third eye
3. Throat (external)
4. Top of shoulders
5. Center of sternum
6. Back of wrists
7. Above belly button (or at belly button through clothes)
8. Pubic bone
9. Root (through clothes)
10. Back of knees
11. Front of ankles
12. Soles of feet

Recommended Resources

▶ YOFA® Essence Waters & YOFA jhe Sessions
www.BeTheMagnet.com/manifest

▶ Rooted in the Infinite - Official YOFA® Text (Look Inside)
www.YOFA.net/rootedintheinfinite

▶ 7 Secrets for Manifesting Your Heart's Desire (Free eCourse)
www.YOFA.net

▶ How to Create a Great Relationship (Free Audio)
www.GreatRelationships.net

▶ Begin Meditating in 3 Minutes (Free Teleseminar Recording)
www.AffirmativeContemplation.com

▶ The Science of Getting Rich (Free ebook)
www.TheScienceofGettingRich.com

▶ The Science of Getting Rich Program (Prosperity Program)
www.YOFA.net/resources/sgr.htm

▶ Mind Movies (Visualization Tool)
www.MindMoviesDiscount.com

▶ Ho'oponopono - Zero Limits (Video Seminar)
www.Hooponopono-ZeroLimits.com

www.ingramcontent.com/pod-product-compliance
Lightning Source LLC
Chambersburg PA
CBHW060638030426
42337CB00018B/3398